EACH THING
WE KNOW
IS CHANGED
BECAUSE
WE KNOW IT

AHSAHTA PRESS

**MODERN AND CONTEMPORARY POETRY
OF THE AMERICAN WEST SERIES**

EACH THING
WE KNOW
IS CHANGED
BECAUSE
WE KNOW IT
AND OTHER POEMS

BY KEVIN HEARLE

BOISE STATE UNIVERSITY • BOISE • IDAHO

Ahsahta Press, Boise State University
Boise, Idaho 83725
http://ahsahtapress.boisestate.edu

ISBN 0-916272-57-5
ISBN-13 978-0-916272-57-9
Library of Congress Catalog Card Number:
93-72424

Acknowledgments:

Crazy River, "Water and Power"; *The Georgia Review,* "Two Composers in Search of One Los Angeles";
The New Orleans Review, "Epistle" and "To Go Home"; *Poetry Flash,* "Earth," "Figure 13f," and
"Sour Grass"; *Quarterly West,* "One Day"; *Seven Poets at Stanford,* Section XII of "Program Notes for
'The Art of Cryptic Postcards'" (as part of "Reminder to Myself"); *The Sonora Review,* "Approaching
the Door" and "West 7th Street"; *Telescope,* "Program Notes for 'The Art of Cryptic Postcards'"
and "The First Demonstration of Muybridge's Zoepraxiscope"; *The University of Windsor Review*
(Canada), "Fire," "Harvest," and "In Memoriam"; *The Yale Review,* "Each Thing We Know Is Changed
Because We Know It."

The author also wishes to thank The Peninsula Community Foundation and The Millay Colony for
the Arts, Inc. for their assistance.

Editor for Ahsahta Press: Dale K. Boyer

Contents

Introduction

". . .the lone shoe in the fast lane."
—Henri Coulette

Thoreau says somewhere in one of his essays, "California is New England's child, bred and board at her school." He did not say it was a good child, but then, for Thoreau, it was the behavior of the parents that was the issue.

All places are complicated, because what one becomes depends on them, but I think poets who are native Californians have bewildering ironic relationships to the place, and not just because California has changed. It's that there are references so strange, so odd, one feels he couldn't explain them to anyone. Who knows, or could care, that one of my family's cherished legends had to do with Sontag and Evans, ranchers who had lost their land due to the exorbitant shipping rates charged by the railroad, and who, in aging retaliation, became excellent train robbers? There are whispered histories too hilarious and naïve to be recorded: my family's distant relatives and their friends (who still ran cattle in the Sierras when the country was young), gathering to defend against the annexation of water in Owens Valley by Los Angeles. They finally decide the best course of action was to take their shotguns and block off the roads leading into the Owens Valley, and . . . just wait for them, the state commissioners and their lawyers, to *try* something. By then, of course, the lawyers and officials didn't need to come anywhere near Owens Valley in order to create, just by adding water, the city of Los Angeles.

Kevin Hearle has written a wonderful book of poems. Its real distinguishment is a kind of belated innocence or "radical innocence" that makes actual wonder possible again. Like Didion or Hass, he is obsessed by an identity that doesn't exist in the world of others, a place (is identity possible without a place?) that doesn't exist anyway now, something that can't be expressed. Every representation of it, in Hearle's work, is another dilemma, for no one is more exiled than a native of the place, especially when he's home.

> And Stravinsky used that one belief
> to change Los Angeles to music.
> He even used my grandmother's four rented rooms:
> each pair of scissors she thought had been stolen
> became, through metaphor,
> dynamic markings—crescendo
> and decrescendo; her marbles—
> aggies, clearies, pee-wees,
> and the ones with the swirls inside,
> the ones that spun the light as they moved—

Later in the poem she replies:

On the table,
her hand-lettered sign, an oboe solo—
KLEPTOMANIACS AND OTHER THIEVES
I AM A CHILD OF GOD—
became a theme like loss
or paranoia, swallowing lesser themes,
became less like loss

. . . . . .

until finally it was so thin
that it was memory,
only another part of the pattern—
or legend—in which Stravinsky
and Schoenberg could live
in Los Angeles for the same eleven years
and somehow never meet.

The innocence here, the innocence recovered by the poet from what might have been only irony, or merely irony, is figured in splendor and loss.

But not judgment. The surviving twin who returns home to San Pedro in "Approaching the Door" finds his mother "two years dead, his father/buried in their massive housekeeper,/ the one who never dusted or made beds,/the former circus fat lady gone too thin,/who then tried to make it with tatoos" is not about to make moral accusations, for there is tacit understanding in this work that is too late for that, that what is important is to notice the maid in all her mouldy, aging vitality. Hearle simply presents the scene, one in which any evaluation of it would be irrelevant and ridiculous *kitsch*.

"You can't say it that way anymore," says Ashbery, and whereas Lowell could rant in his early work like some avenging Puritan against the corruption of the country generally, Hearle, in 1994, is left only with the final product of a culture in which the Puritan impulse became the acquisitive one. In this regard, he is the only poet I can think of who has written an invective against lawns, one that is every bit as bitter as it is funny. And yet, in a culminating poem, "On Being Hurried Through the Prado," Hearle shows us that "you can still say it that way" if you travel back far enough to claim it as yours. It's a curiously moving poem, in which the poet finds his identity by leaving his place, finds himself doubled and mirrored in the figure of his "madrileño friend," Rafael,who rushes him through the Prado "as if it didn't matter, or as if/it mattered more than I could understand"—exactly what Hearle feels about his place, about his history. As he is rushed through the museum, Hearle recalls a cogstone "plowed up on the land/along the river we once called ours." What he isolates here is that complicated sense of exile, even usurpation, that the native of the place must feel. California belongs to others now. That's quite a loss, quite a *hubris* that goes before it, too. What the poet decides he wants, there in the Prado, is to turn away and be transfigured by a pain larger than his own. What the poem finds is tragedy, not moral judgment.

I wanted then

to spend my years in a deserted room
of Goya's darkest works: the soldier's boots;
their heads inclined over their row of rifles;
the unarmed dead; and those waiting to die,

alive with individual motions;
the clutch of grief, the one man, his arms open
to the light—defiant there on the background
of this eternal night of May the 3rd,

1808 along a wall in Madrid,
where the painting still hangs as a reminder
that its homeland has been a place of conquest
and murder, perhaps a place, somewhat like Thebes,

not to be entered lightly. Thebes, where Freud
discovered Oedipus' riddled life:
the primal violence of fathers, sons,
and silence ending in self-blinded kings.

There is a cunning involved in the phrasing toward the end of this: for a moment the poem, so discursive, so referential, almost seems to digress, to trail off into Thebes. But it is impossible to forget that Spain and California have both been places of conquest and murder, and at this point Hearle's privately invested history in the place of his birth is humbled, shown to be part of the tragic, "self-blinded" history of all places in Western culture. What is magical in its authority here is the way the poet recovers the feeling (as if he has merely kept it in abeyance for a moment) in that final line. The issue isn't that "self-blinded" kings is shockingly original. It's that it isn't. What is shocking is the "silence ending" and its implications, for what follows the silence is a king, blinded and howling in pain. Like Goya's etchings in which the muzzle of the executioner's gun appears at the edge, the condemned man pleading for his life in the foreground, the "silence ending" here halts the action just as it is meant to.

What we listen for at the end of the poem is what humbles us, for the blind king is the end of all power, the place where we don't own anything anymore. The art of the poem withholds the howling so that we can only imagine its sound as our own, although we will not hear it. This is the difficult art of restraint, the brilliantly withheld moment in which the quick rhythm of the final line stops time.

This is a brilliant first book, not because the poet is a native Californian troubled by his sense of exile from his place even though he lives there. It's brilliant because the poet is so gifted. By the end of it Hearle sees through his illusions and cherished self enchantments, has seen through himself, so that his book, at the end, looks out on the world.

Larry Levis
Richmond, Virginia
February, 1994

For Libby

EACH
THING
WE
KNOW

Each Thing We Know Is Changed Because We Know It

A eucalyptus has its implications
where I come from: it means the autumn winds
return each year like brushfires from the desert,
return as dry reminders of the oaks
whose place this was: the valley oak, blue oak,
and the oracle which thrive on little water.
And eucalyptus means the orange groves
once flourished here, that rivers were diverted,
that winter was denied and smoke hung low
over the valley the night of the first frost—
smudgepots warming and darkening the sky.
And eucalyptus means that people lived here;
the flesh tones of the mottled trunk, the bark
in strips that dry and curl and fall to the ground
mean that my mother's family would walk,
through walnut orchards and orange groves, to church—
Saturday nights, three women, three generations,
bound for the revival meeting, each collecting
more friends as she went further south through town.
And eucalyptus leaves, silver, scythe-like,
shaken down by the wind, the tree still tall,
scented the questions that my mother asked
when her senile grandmother would get out
of the house, walk south through the orchards, south
right through downtown, straight to the water tower.
Dark letters spilled across it six foot tall—
SANTA ANA SANTA ANA, high

and circular, the water named the town.
Great-grandmother would stand beneath it—no words
she could recall to call herself—just waiting,
for what she didn't know, and trying on names.

Two Composers in Search of One Los Angeles

I
Schoenberg understood the suburbs—
half-screams and jabbering glissandos.
In a sequence without tradition,
out of pieces with no past,
each note created equal—
a terrible new music:
neighbors from Dubuque and Buffalo
becoming instant Californians.

Each of his notes an orphan,
himself in exile, a pariah,
Schoenberg understood L.A.
as alienation:
the town drunk come forward to be saved
at the altar of his town
and of his Lord, there on his knees
asking forgiveness, which, outside
after they have passed the plate,
after the last *Amen*, when he is sober,
he knows the town will never give.
He will read judgment in their eyes:
their stares when he's not looking,
their sideways glances when he is,
all call him drunk, call him stranger—
each look nailing him shut, his soul outside of theirs.
Then, walking through the walnut orchards,

he will curse the stars because they are predictable,
and because tomorrow he will be drunk,
and, hanging from a parking meter on Grand,
he will call out greetings to nervous relatives
who only half understand
this thing they call forgiveness.

Los Angeles was in his music
not as a place, but as
a separation—
tabula rasa for his soul.

II
Stravinsky understood cities
as aggregates: Bertolt Brecht;
Howard Hughes; my father learning
to swear from Carole Lombard
as he sat on Will Rodgers' knee;
Aldous Huxley down the block
from Thomas Mann. Stravinsky,
he knew that archaeologists
measure cultures from what they throw away,
and so he used it all:
Georgie Yeats in a trance on a train
from San Berdoo to the City of Angels,
the spirits speaking through her as the train,
passing through orange groves and chaparral,

bore William Butler Yeats toward the question,
What are you here for?
They didn't ask the question back;
they answered, *We have come*
to give you metaphors for poetry.
And Stravinsky used that one belief
to change Los Angeles to music.
He even used my grandmother's four rented rooms:
each pair of scissors she thought had been stolen
became, through metaphor,
dynamic markings—crescendo
and decrescendo; her marbles—
aggies, clearies, pee-wees,
and the ones with the swirl inside,
the ones that spun the light as they moved—
became grace notes almost lost
among the clatter of egg cartons,
painted rocks, old photographs,
and cottage cheese tops. On the table,
her hand-lettered sign, an oboe solo—
KLEPTOMANIACS AND OTHER THIEVES
I AM A CHILD OF GOD—
became a theme like loss
or paranoia, swallowing lesser themes,
becoming less like loss
and more like the D.A.R. the more it grew,
until finally it was so thin

that it was memory,
only another part of the pattern—
or legend—in which Stravinsky
and Schoenberg could live
in Los Angeles for the same eleven years
and somehow never meet.

One Day

Sometimes it seems everything happened
during the summer that it rained and the greenhouse
sat skewed across the thin front lawn—the summer sky,
and each plastic window, a momentary sheet
of hothouse glare, both blinding and transparent,
through which the world was changed.
I learned to read that year;
perhaps Kennedy was shot; and I, dreaming
of Sandy Koufax, collected papers for the school paper drive.
It couldn't have happened the way I remember,
except that the sky was close to the trees that day,
and I had filled the greenhouse with papers past my head;
a five year old growing a stack of time and a list
of neighborhood widows—their aprons and quiet garages,
boxes and bundles, mildewed and sad.
Only Koufax on the radio could rise
above the hot, pitched roof of heaven, and read
perfection in the news. I fumbled through the bundles
searching for his name, wanting to be him.
When Churchill died, a man knocked on the door
and offered us a truckload more of papers for the lawn;
Dad said I had enough but thank you. Still, we lost;
and it rained that day from 1:05 to 1:15—
the slow, heavy drops spotting the driveway and sidewalk
before the air lightened—and that one day
in a dry season was more than I could understand.

Approaching the Door

He thought he heard his mother's death cries,
moans that had filled the harbor at San Pedro
with the fear of a poisoned birth, his brother,
David the stillborn, who'd rocked in the tides
of his mother's womb and had drunk deeply
of the peritonitis that had killed them both,
one turning color inside the other;
he thought he heard all that again, and rising
in darkness, his feet in the hollow hall
seemed to make a plangent noise
upon the cold, unyielding floor
as he, wanting to comfort her
and needing her comfort, approached her door
still in dreams of *You'll be fine, Mama.*
Please, you'll be fine. But he opened the door
to find his mother two years dead, his father
buried in their massive housekeeper,
the one who never dusted or made beds,
the former circus fat lady gone too thin
who'd then tried to make it with tattoos,
the one whose steaming dragon thigh
was breathing fire upon his father
as she screamed for help in carny slang, *Hey Rube,*
Hey Rube, Oh God, I'm coming now. Hey Rube.

Hunchback Sundays

Black shoes in the House of the Lord, black shoes.
Though Christ was barefoot throughout Sunday School
I wore God's heavy shoes—small, black, and corrective—
and rode beside my grandmother to church,
watching her upstretched arms reach for the wheel
which, as she drove would circumscribe her face—
an aureole made in Detroit for her;
and, therefore, unlike those of other saints
whose feet had never pawed the air to reach
the pedals of their cars. Her own back halo
more solid that the Christ's whose back was so straight,
so perfect, that I never understood
exactly how she came to love him so.

West 7th Street

In childhood, cruelty was a separate language, as was the Spanish
that Jeepie and Yolanda spoke to their Mexican grandmother
who muttered those grave, inconsolable syllables to her shoes,
and when she looked up you understood and ran away; and cruelty
was like the solar eclipse the summer that old Packard,
parked down the block long before your time, and inexplicable,
exploded into flames under the date palm—your parents told you
not to look, but it was there: the cold, hollow sun and the dark;
or maybe it was like the birthday parties they had across the
    street
with the burro piñatas slung with ropes from the second story
and the children taking their turns with the incised bat and the
    blindfold,
each one wanting it to swing low, full of their need to break it
    open;
yes, it must have been like that—all that sweetness hanging in
    the air
and kids just swinging wildly.

The Lesson

for Hazel Greenleaf Flaherty

When my shoulders shook
you told me how, when you were three
meningitis had curled

your spine. You held
my strange, unruly hands.
The doctors hadn't thought you would live.

It became an incantation:
The doctors don't know
everything. You will be normal

someday. Normal. We sat
on the lower bunk
repeating the cross, the pulls,

the tucks, and all the loops
I'd memorized as dread
and as failure. Repeated

for three years, for an hour
each day, one knee
tucked up under my chin,

it became an act
of creation: this fumbling
at myself, and the dust motes

spangling and shaping the light
as it sank—a material thing—
to the wood slat floor.

You told me you'd died once;
that looking up you'd seen
a light you had known

must have been God—
binding and bright—
lifting you out of yourself.

Looking down then
you'd seen your question mark
body on the table.

The doctors had been so
frantic, so normal there,
calling you back

to the particular
boundaries of the flesh,
that you had smiled, and let them

pull you back. I tie
my shoes by instinct now—
my mind giving itself

up to the common world
of things—but, if I think
about the movements, then

I remember you, I
slow down, and, once again,
these are my hands.

Sour Grass

Your mother hates the stuff. She blames some great-
great aunt, and can't forget the day John Sherwin
pulled the dead cow out of his family's barn.
It had turned blue a bit, and green some places.
Your mother and her friends thought that was more
than spectacle enough for them, and walked
down Flower Street toward the old pepper tree
they played in after school. They saw her then,
Amanda Greenleaf, your great-grandmother,

gray-haired and loony, going door-to-door
selling sour grass. Your mother and grandmother
spent most of Sundays that year visiting
at the State Hospital. They found her once
up on the shelf, crouched in her small, dark closet;
her eyes, all crazed with light, glaring at them
like a hoot owl's. That day of the dead cow,
well after she'd deposited Amanda
safely at home, your mother's friends told her

insanity's hereditary, and
she never showed you the small yellow flowers
planted by that bad painter great-great aunt
along the banks of irrigation ditches.
Perhaps she was thinking of her own mother,
a hunchbacked genealogist who planted
whole yards without permission: plum pits, roses,

geraniums and carrots—good intentions
spreading like weeds to water in a dry land.

The family eyes, still shifting hazel, stare
at your mother now through you, who love the past
almost as much as your grandmother did
who read your future in the gypsy's cards—
her emphasis on wishes. She showed you how
to savor green and sour, to chew the stalk,
that long impressionist green shaft of growth,
until you too felt redolent with light—
luminous—tasting the odd liberty of weeds.

SHATTERS
INTO
SONG

Earth

The black asphalt cul-de-sacs of summer days
were never kinder than when the heat rose,
languid in its distortion, and we kids
kicked off our shoes to cross that brilliant street—
heel to toe, heel to toe—sweating to see
who could go slowest, who could plant his feet
until they seemed extensions of that place:
the hard, the creeping heat, all black, all rising;
and then the other children running, running
to leave you there in your own ritual,
your small feet burning in the road. Oh happy
the child who furnishes his soul with pain.

Epistle

Music coming from an open window. Sitting in the courtyard—
an abundance of windows, a square of blue, a tree—

the wind, the sunlight, and your fingers
flashing like the scissors in my hair. On my bare shoulders

the hair falls, fragrant as leaves in pools. Linda,
wherever you are, your name means *beautiful*;

someone should have been in love with you
who cut our hair for a rose and a first class stamp.

I'm sending this *general delivery/world* to tell you
today I trimmed my beard:

the water washing the short hairs off my arm
was like the wind in sunshine;

surprised, I saw my mouth open in the mirror—
my tongue and two lips blossoming

into *Linda*.

Air

for Leo Patrick Flaherty

When the Santa Ana winds blow,
I know this is the air you came here for

from far off, mythical Cleveland,
from the steel mills along Lake Erie

among whose furnaces and raging storms
of coal ash, wind and melting snow

you were the one consumed, until
in the sanatarium in paradise

you met your bride—that strange,
mis-shapen angel who was your nurse.

For five years, you were engaged. Was
it the consummation that you feared—the blood

spread upon the sheets; her tender, grotesque
innocence and your last breath gasped out as one?

You didn't live to know there was a child
you'd helped conceive, born in a town

now famous for the wind which sweeps away
the L.A. smog, a haze which is the air

of millions. Your daughter is a mother now
to sons from that same city, who can

in the fall, in a week of changing winds, breathe
both the air you came here for, and the air you left behind.

Trivia Californiana: Looking at a Seashell While in Iowa
September 9, 1982

A skillful archaeologist can trace
the movement of a culture from a cowry,
bits of obsidian, or abalone.
This is my oldest, favorite shell from childhood.
I found it in a sheltered cove at low tide,
and picked it up. The animal was dead,
and so I claimed the purplish Coffee Bean,
half-inch *Trivia Californiana.*

A Jesuit discovered from a shell
of abalone that cartographers
were wrong, that California was no island.
He knew that abalone only lived
on the Pacific side of California,
so, when Mojave Indians gave Kino
blue shells in Arizona, he knew Baja
was a peninsula. He proved the Gulf

in 1702 by walking south
and west with a sick friend until they saw
sunrise over the water. His friend died.
Kino mapped the north end of the Gulf
of California, mapped the hard connection
between the island of their myths and charts
and the Mojave Desert. Kino mapped
the route he and his friend had taken there.

I am not a surveyor, but I know
just how to rock a two-legged sifting tray
so that the waste slips through the gauge, not out
over the side; so that the scrapers, shards
of pottery, charcoal and chipping waste,
and the few points, stand out revealed in air.
From its radial cracks, I know a stone
that has been worked from one that's merely worn.

Across two thousand miles of quavering
phone lines my mother's voice cracks. She is
the oldest generation now. And tired.
Mignonette Amanda Greenleaf Richmond,
my mother's aunt, ninety years old, is dead.
Although she loved the ocean, circumstances
kept her inland among the mining claims,
foothills, and orchards of the Mother Lode.

But no, this shell's too small to be a cowry.
It would confuse an archaeologist
to find it here. And she died in Riverside,
miles from the sea, in Riverside, swept by
the tidal wrack of L.A. smog. She's dead.
There's nothing to remind me of her here,
except my memory itself, this shell,
and what I know of trade routes from the sea.

Shaped to its purpose, sharper than the air
of that high desert town at apple harvest,
fifteen millimeter birdpoint

for which perhaps a man had once gone hungry
trading food to get chalcedony.
And thinking then of quail, he'd cooked the stone

and stared into the coals—each small sun burning
on the ground of night—until, the fire all cold
and thin at dawn, the hot chalcedony

stone cooled—glassy as obsidian,
but white. And then he struck it; felt the light
reflected in his hand both wane and sharpen;

chipping away until he had a core
ready to be transformed into a weapon.
On that fall afternoon, I offered them,

reluctantly, this point—so beautiful
in my twelve-year-old hand—which was not mine,
so I could see it published without guilt.

Fire

Burning in a saint's wind in the dry bed
of her dry river, fires here are like the wind;
the wind here is like a flame. It can carry fire
from hilltop to hilltop across a canyon—
a living thing then, carnivorous,
it drinks the air; it swallows whole the land;
and grows—the wind creating flames; the flames,
creating wind, explode through the chamise,
igniting the red shanks and yerba santa.
Everything that is holy burns, or is carried
in the wind, or on the winter rain, to the sea.

Harvest

Hands black and sweet and sticky in the fall;
hulling the walnuts, picking the persimmons.
Climbing the trees the fruit would be so ripe
and taut with light against the sky that sometimes
my tugging at a branch to pick one fruit
would free another persimmon higher up;
it would be so beautiful mid-air,
a sweet light breaking through transparent flesh,
that I would try to catch it as it fell,
if only to stain my hands with its bursting.

Water and Power

It is true that nearly 40 percent of Los Angeles' water goes for outside uses such as lawns, gardens, swimming pools, and public parks . . . but such amenities are at the heart of Los Angeles' way of life.
—Remi Nadeau

Despite your thousand pious gigolo suburbs;
and even though I know the lies the angels tell the living
in Los Angeles—the way history eclipses history here
and passes into fable—this is my heritage: the land of the lawn
and the home of the sprinkler head. Oh, I have wasted my time
detesting the soap kings and the chewing gum barons—
so much time on the real estate men planning their floral parades
and football games. They were nothing;
each one mortal and pitiful. It is the lawn which has survived,
and which I hate. I do not think they would have come—
the bacon and ham millionaires of Illinois,
the five and dime rich merchants of Ohio—if
there hadn't been lawns for the making. Without dichondra
they would not have boarded the Pullman cars for Pasadena
or Santa Barbara. If not for the sprinkler heads,
which made an arid land seem green and neatly divisible,
the railroad speculators could not have brought Iowa west,
in square lots, to the Pacific. And, without the millions
from Cedar Falls and Council Bluffs and Keokuk,
the banks would not have come—like locusts over Egypt—
with their New Yorkers spreading legends of a lost city
of true intelligence, benevolence, culture
and pastrami. The apostles of the Empire State
rehearsing their litany of things which were *better back there,*

but entering their whiny exile in ever greater numbers,
and each one wanting lawns. Never mind the seasons without rain
or the water wasted on St. Augustine; they must have lawns.
Lawns, so the people, we, the people, can move on
(each moving van an absolution), believing
in new towns whose names sound more chaste—"Mission Viejo";
in offramps more green—"Ventura," "Garden Grove";
and in—"Salsipuedes," "Los Feliz"—lives perhaps
more sibilant than what we've left behind.
Damn the lawns. Damn the sprinkler heads which feed them.
Damn the pipes and aqueducts that feed the sprinklers
that feed the lawns that feed the thirst for green and land,
and damn the dams which feed on river valleys so far away
voracious angels need never dream they once were green.

The Politics of Memory

I was born in a state
where everything had to be named twice
to survive:
where Hangtown became Placerville,
where La Brea couldn't hold its bones
in Spanish, but had to be redundant
and bi-lingual—
The La Brea Tar Pits,
redundant, like the Sierra Nevada Mountains,
in name only;

a state so arid in parts
that what has been forgotten
is blown to dust
in the wind across the alkali flats;
a state where you change the name
and all is forgiven:
where Gospel Swamp
loses both its muck and its religion
to emerge the model suburb.

Fountain Valley forgives the swamp,
but what of Manzanar?
In a state where everything
has to be named twice
or be forgotten,
who will remember Manzanar

(a place in exile
from the maps)? The detention camp is closed,
but I was born into this state,
and, for now, I know the name.

In Memoriam

John Logan 1923-1987

A fall,

his tongue raging
at itself, creating
(such loneliness—

his mother, dead
in childbirth)
the words and memory

stolen from him by stroke;
his breath too soft now,
then too hard; his lips

stunned by meanings
they could not convey;
his palsied hand

and arm no longer a support,
he saw the earth approaching
and kissed it

uncontrollably.

To Go Home

Yossarian, Yossarian,
you and I, we never met, Yossarian.
I am the son of the granddaughter
of the crazy woman whose tree you must have circled—
shadow in training 1942
in Santa Ana, in California,
before you knew insanity was real
and institutional. I don't believe
in Christ or God, and so I pray to you,
the raucous shape of fiction, circling
not the barn, leaning into old age, suspended
among wisteria, but navigating
upon the thirty-six-foot trunk, and the branches
bent to earth by their own weight and age.
Yossarian, imaginary bombs,
oracular and silent, fall from your eyes,
burning the clouds of feral blue wisteria,
dismembering the Greenleaf family tree,
a massive California pepper,
and flattening the groves
of orange, walnut, and persimmon.
Oh bombardier, such was your practice run;
your wings they cast the hours upon our land.
Too many pilots, too many bombardiers;
it was all gone before I could be born;
no shade from which my grandmother
first saw her grandmother—only legends,

old words without direction running around
lost in the subdivisions—no apple tree
the neighbor's horse would run to when loose,
no irrigation ditches fringed with the weeds
Aunt Franny sowed, no nothing,
nothing to bear them witness, and no place,
no, no place left, for them to plant their sorrow.
Yossarian, you must be crazy to go home.

Blue Willow Pattern

Beneath the teacup sky, tipped
upside down and spun around three times,
we are the wish, the tea leaves, and our fortune.

Perhaps the gypsy apricot picker/
reader of cards foretold this:
in the sixth year of Eisenhower

in a town named for the river
with a name for the wind
that blows through the City of Angels

on the shore of the Bay of Smokes,
a child will be born to love
the queen of clubs—

a light skinned, dark haired woman.
Such ease to claim our lives are fated,
and such reduction. I have chosen this.

My once general wish for love, cupped
in my aunt's willowware could not have
conceived of or accommodated us.

At dawn, the still tree,
filled with sleeping birds, shatters
into song; I wake, and you rise

to all my senses.

THE
WORK
OF
THE
PAST

For Confucius, Giordano Bruno, and my Uncle Johnie

I sing this song for Confucius,
who loved music and recommended it
as a means of moderating grief;
    and I sing this song
for Giordano Bruno, who
loved memory and felt
    that nothing
was ever moderated—it was
transposed into a different form;
    and I sing
this song for my Uncle Johnie,
who, in his love and
    drunkenness
at eighty-two, called me
his grandson and begged me
    to remember his dreams.
I cannot please them all:
I remember their dreams
    only so much
as they are mine, and I sing
to remember them, those
    who made me who I am.
And, if I should wake up
from their dreams no longer singing,
    that would be the grief
    most wholly mine.

On Being Hurried Through The Prado

This perennial rebirth, this fluidity of American life . . .
—F. J. Turner

Rafael, my madrileño friend,
had laughed at California's landmarks,
at how each generation feels it must
reclaim the land before it is its own.

Now, quoting from *The Book of the Perplexed*—
how Moses led the twelve tribes helter-skelter
around the desert in circles on purpose,
because they needed a full forty years

to prepare themselves for the holy land—
he rushed me through the Prado in one morning
as if it didn't matter, or as if
it mattered more than I could understand.

One time I'd shown him, innocently enough,
the cogstone, hewn for purposes unknown,
above my mother's desk—a doughnut shape
her great-grandfather'd plowed up on the land

along the river which we once called ours.
Turning a corner onto the netherlandish
City of Hell burning inside *The Garden
of Earthly Delights*, I wanted to move in

that world of galleries (not quickly through it),
to understand the eggshell lusts of Bosch,

the courtly draftsmanship Velazquez painted,
and all El Greco's rapture. I wanted then

to spend my years in a deserted room
of Goya's darkest works: the soldiers' boots;
their heads inclined over their row of rifles;
the unarmed dead; and those waiting to die,

alive with individual motions:
the clutch of grief, the one man his arms open
to the light—defiant there on the background
of this eternal night of May the 3rd,

1808 along a wall in Madrid,
where the painting still hangs as a reminder
that its homeland has been a place of conquest
and murder, perhaps a place, somewhat like Thebes,

not to be entered lightly. Thebes, where Freud
discovered Oedipus' riddled life:
the primal violence of fathers, sons,
and silence ending in self-blinded kings.

Las Meninas

after Michel Foucault

Velazquez painted himself in a corner,
barely inside the arc of light. He stares
at us: the outside royalty implied
by his strict vision, and the stares of dwarves
and other courtiers. The stretcher bars
and canvas back are all that we can see
of his portrait of us; and even he
has poised the oils in his left hand, brush frozen
in his right, to look at us before, once more,
returning to the materials of his art.

Our daughter, the Infanta, stands in the center
of her retainers—facing out forever,
oblivious to the profiles watching her
watch for us through El Escorial
in vain. Velazquez leaned his lesson well:
The image should stand out from the frame
was what Pacheco told him in Seville;
and that we do, old painter, that we do.

No one sees us the way we see us, although
we rise above our daughter's head, behind her
in silver—in the mirror no one sees;
not even that elusive lord behind them
on the stairs. They don't notice him. He sees
all that there is to see, and is prepared
to either leave or enter; but he stays
outside the room, holding the curtain open.

Reading *The Master Forger*

Han van Meegeren, 1899-1947
for Clive Delbridge

Because a painting dries out over time,
leaving the forms of colors hard (resistant
after fifty years to most solvents),
van Meegeren had to have an oil to mix
his pigments with which wouldn't frizzle or
discolor paint when baked. It took four years
of cooking oils out of test canvases
before the forger found his great solution
in oil of lilacs. Legend has it that
he came to love the necessary lilacs,
but it's more likely they were camouflage,
that even as he baked their essence hard
the fragrant flowers fooled his visitors.

For his first forgery, "Christ at Emmaus,"
he resurrected an old, undistinguished
"Lazarus," scraped the paint off—except the lead-
based white which was too solid to remove
(he built a table setting out of it
in the foreground)—and painted over a spot
beside Christ's head. I hear you in your story,
Uncle, "Vermeer perfected realism.
From his materials he learned technique:
blues he crushed from lapis lazuli,
cinnabar ground into vermilion dust,
another red he brayed from cochineal—
which is quicksilver mixed with brimstone . . . ."

Crossing the street that night, there was a car—
in my tears, two beacons, then a swarm of light
surrounding me. I stopped. And then the darkness
as the car swerved. "Help me. Someone please help me,"
I cried. For a year I crossed that street each day
laughing at how the others walked across
trusting themselves trusting two painted lines.
I thought I knew how much you must have hurt
to do it, but now I wonder and can't sleep.
Why, Uncle, did they find you on the floor?
"In Han van Meegeren's studio," you'd said,
"he posed himself as model, forged himself
into whatever postures he required,

painting the images he saw in mirrors
and adding faces as they came to him.
His Vermeer forgeries were beautiful,
painted with boar's hair brushes dipped in hues
he crushed by hand. The best museums vied
against each other to buy his fakes.
It was an accident they caught him at all.
After the war, when Goering's stash was found
van Meegeren's name was on the bill of sale
for a Vermeer. Charged with collaboration,
he died on trial with his defense unfinished,
completion of his final forgery
still hanging on that lustre—crackling and

almost insoluble—through which a world's
ideal must shine." No, Uncle. *Painting there*
in court, "The Young Christ Teaching in the Temple"
convicted him. Each stroke was an admission
of his greatness and his guilt. Though I have tried
to tell myself that it was nothing, facing
that car that night has changed my life. It had to.
Why did they find you on the floor? Why?
Was suicide a sloughing off of pain,
or did death stagger you, too late, with life,
that inexplicable desire in you
crouched there in terror, crawling for the phone
to tell this world of lies one final truth?

Drawing

for Libby

Three hours I've drawn you into a mass of gray
erasure marks; because although I know
to draw is to imagine gravity,
the way it climbs the spine, I'm not an artist
who learned, from cutting up the dead, to love
the skeleton—the way a body, falling
upwards, will pull the earth up after it
(ever so slightly) in a dream of flight.
But even wings have weight, and I have tried
these hours to draw your face as if it floated.
What gravity there is for you I feel
as loss, and yet, for me to do you justice,
these lines must bend with weight and rise with effort—
the muscles of the face in flight above
the skull, lifting the mouth into a smile.

Rita, Yasmin and the Mirror

Mother, that's you. Rita. Ree—tah. You.
Her hair is white. Rita's hair.
Look in the mirror. That's your face. Rita's face.
My hair was red. That is not my face. Not Rita's.
Mother . . . Rita . . . in the mirror. Remember?
My hair is black. Remember? Not Rita's.
That's an easy name to forget.
Rita Margarita Carmen Khan Cansino Welles
Gilda Love Goddess Hayworth bombshell star
There never was a girl like Gilda
They named a bomb for Gilda—A Bomb—
black satin striptease of atoms
slipping off electrons, sloughing off identity,
the nuclear gloves coming off . . .
Remember the Alamogordo—
Put the blame on maim, boys
I am become death, destroyer of worlds
in my nightgown, all white satin and black lace,
descending on Hiroshima. The light fantastic,
a light so bright no eye could bear to see it,
tripping and blowing my technicolor hair,
and that pert cloud of hell, all lace and bare shoulders—
I am become death; that's an easy name to forget.
Whose face is that in the mirror?
Maybe I'll live so long that I'll forget her.
Maybe I'll die trying. Publicity.
Hundreds of thousands dead. My name. The photos.

The Most Exciting Girl On The Screen
broke into tears of real gratitude
and then threw up, when they named the bomb for her,
for Gilda, that's an easy girl to forget—
maybe I'll die trying; her husband did
in the funhouse, in the hall of mirrors,
forgetting her one by one, killing the blonde
in one mirror, the brunette in another,
shattering image after image—that's not my face—
one husband murdered me and the other directed him.
I don't want to be within a thousand miles of that city,
or any other city, when they start dropping those bombs.
But that's not my face. That's not my name.
I am become forgetting; there never was a girl like me.
That was not my bomb.

The First Demonstration of Muybridge's Zoepraxiscope
Palo Alto Stock Farm 1879

The mind when shown a horse in one position
will hold it there, ignoring all the gaps
which aren't the horse, until it reappears
further along its gallop—this is called
persistence of vision, and continues as long
as the hooves pound upon the retina
so fast the memory cannot recall
remembering. Great speed is necessary
or this delusion fails—perception changes—
revealing that once great horse, Occident,
to be a lunging beast; unbalanced there
on film: his left foreleg curling under him,
his right, extended straight, reaches the turf.
Only at this speed, when the myth of motion stops,
can we see clearly with what steps the horse runs,
and analyze his gait, the litany
of hoof and fetlock, as the perfect flow
of discontinuities. Unmoving, graceless,
and powerful, the horse strains in each frame
for the fragile equilibrium
in which each step reconstitutes his form.

Program Notes for "The Art of Cryptic Postcards"

I

There is an art to writing postcards:
while you drive at 55, you freeze frame thoughts
and claim great knowledge just in passing.
This picture's of Flaming Gorge, Wyoming.
Notice the jade green water against
the autumn colors of the cliff walls.
Remember: *The Green River meanders*
through scenic Flaming Gorge. Notice the sky
is a hieroglyphic blue. Scrupulous
in its perfection. It's timeless in my memory,
because I've never been to the river there.
This is what postcards were meant to be.

II

Before every photograph
there is a negative which forms
the burnt ground of it perceptions,
and turns them the autumn shades: fire, leaves,
coals and ash. The dark side
of a photograph is solid and still.
What we see in a picture is the result
of acids and frozen time, and whatever
light that we bring to it.

III

Musicians call it an appogiatura:
an ambiguous note, neither tonic
nor dominant, it may signal discord
or foreshadow a new movement
with a Minor fall into more distant
harmonies expressive of desire—
the need for meaning become sensual
and aching in the distance.

IV

In Arnold Schoenberg's twelve-tone scale
the principle of order is the series;
harmony is rejected as an old habit
of piling notes together, is rejected
as a logical flow: the whole cannot
be greater than the sum of the parts.
Each note in Schoenberg is theoretically
equivalent, and requires no metaphysics
or sentimentality to join it to the rest.

Therefore, in this section the chorus all sprechstimme:
                    To remember for a reason
                     is to mix memory with desire
                      and give them both a meaning,
as if each note were an appoggiatura.

V

Three times she crossed forgetfulness' waters:
she drank the Lethe's draught regretfully
the first time; next, she only crossed the waters;
but the third time she drank it hungrily
and to the last. So she could be his prize,
a man she hadn't known had charmed the Queen
to tears by singing songs. And her surprise
was that she'd loved the poet, half unseen,
who'd sung for her past Cerberus and Charon,
and that she'd feared their passage, and his back,
rising in joy to meet the setting sun
until she'd asked, *Who are you?* He'd gone slack;
and, as he'd turned to her in grief, she'd known
that in his turning around his grief had grown.

VI

"It's a poor sort of memory
That only works backwards," the Queen remarked.

VII

Sprechstimme is a method of singing
which Schoenberg invented. In it a note,
or tone, is struck and then slid away from
by the singer, as if no perfect moment
or tone could last, or as if perfection
didn't exist. It's marked by an X,

as on a treasure map, and by empty spots,
flags, black spots, and their indications
of a note's length, weight, and value.
It is an eerie singing,
akin to both music and speech.

VIII
Pity the poor maidens of Thrace.
Orpheus lived in the past and sang
only of his Eurydice, never of them.
Finally, one drunken day
they tried to stone him; but
the stones they flung from their slender hands,
missiles when thrown, became a garland—
the charmed stones stopping mid-air
to praise his song before they fell
softly at his feet. The maidens then—
too much rejection
mixed with their wine—screamed
until the weak-willed stones
forgot the song they could no longer hear
and killed him. Each maiden claimed
her souvenir: one loved his thigh,
another his right hand; but
the poor girl who picked his head
found out, too late,
the damn thing wouldn't stop singing.

Disgusted, she threw his head
away into the river.

IX
In 1785, while the world
celebrated what scientists called
its five thousand seven hundred
and eighty-ninth birthday,
James Hutton contemplated Scotch rocks;
and what he saw in schist and sandstone
was the immensity of time
in the cycles of the earth: uplift,
and erosion, creation upon creation
beyond imagining—*no vestige*
of a beginning, no prospect of an end.

X
Today's the day that never was
and never will be. Here,
wherever it may be,
is the center of the world.
But music is not memory.
Arnold Schoenberg was not Orpheus.
Photography is not a stone.

XI

Things which are set in stone
are often sedimentary,
and contradictory
in that each generation builds
upon the work of the past
and the decay of the present,
yet still believes in progress.
Their names have numbers to them.

Igneous rocks are large, hot-tempered
builders of worlds. Splashy extroverts
or massively repressed islands
of stone in a world of wind and rain
and from above something always
weighing you down. Traditionally,
they avoid sentimental meetings
such as clubs and family reunions.

The metamorphic rocks
have undergone sea change,
or changed identities
because the heat was on
or the pressure got too much
for them—the riddlers, liars,
amnesiacs, and freaks
whose favorite con, unchanging,

is to let you think
you can identify them
with something else.

XII
Still I think of fabled Orpheus
and the shore which he last passed with eyes long dead
and head still hanging as if to stop the stones.

About the Author

Kevin Hearle was born on St. Patrick's Day, 1958, in Santa Ana, California, the second of three sons of a family whose mother's side had come to California during the Gold Rush and had moved south to Santa Ana in 1871. His congenital defects of the hips and legs were corrected in infancy, but he was an awkward and self-conscious child. He earned a bachelor's degree in English, with Distinction, in 1980 from Stanford University, and an MFA in English from the Writers' Workshop at the University of Iowa in 1983. In November 1983 he married Elizabeth "Libby" Hearle. Returning to California in 1984, he earned a Ph.D. in Literature in December 1991 from the University of California at Santa Cruz. This book was a finalist for the National Poetry Series and the Yale Series of Younger Poets in 1992, and individual poems were nominated for the Pushcart Prize and appeared in numerous anthologies, including *California Poetry: from the Gold Rush to the Present, The Poetry Cure,* and *Unfolding Beauty: Celebrating California's Landscapes.*

Hearle was the revision editor for the Viking Critical Library second edition of *The Grapes of Wrath: Text and Criticism,* and the co-editor of *Beyond Boundaries: Rereading John Steinbeck.* He received the Burkhardt Award as the Outstanding Steinbeck Scholar of the Year in 2005. He has been an adjunct faculty member at the University of Iowa, Coe College, San Jose State University, University of California at Santa Cruz, California State University at Los Angeles, Notre Dame de Namur University and Santa Clara University. He lives with his wife on the San Francisco Peninsula.

Ahsahta Press

SAWTOOTH POETRY PRIZE SERIES

2002: Aaron McCollough, *Welkin* (Brenda Hillman, judge)
2003: Graham Foust, *Leave the Room to Itself* (Joe Wenderoth, judge)
2004: Noah Eli Gordon, *The Area of Sound Called the Subtone* (Claudia Rankine, judge)
2005: Karla Kelsey, *Knowledge, Forms, The Aviary* (Carolyn Forché, judge)

NEW SERIES

1. Lance Phillips, *Corpus Socius*
2. Heather Sellers, *Drinking Girls and Their Dresses*
3. Lisa Fishman, *Dear, Read*
4. Peggy Hamilton, *Forbidden City*
5. Dan Beachy-Quick, *Spell*
6. Liz Waldner, *Saving the Appearances*
7. Charles O. Hartman, *Island*
8. Lance Phillips, *Cur aliquid vidi*
9. Sandra Miller, *Oriflamme*
10. Brigitte Byrd, *Fence Above the Sea*
11. Ethan Paquin, *The Violence*
12. Ed Allen, *67 Mixed Messages*
13. Brian Henry, *Quarantine*
14. Kate Greenstreet, *case sensitive*
15. Aaron McCollough, *Little Ease*

Ahsahta Press

Modern and Contemporary Poetry of the American West

This book is set in Apollo MT type with Frutiger Black Condensed titles
by Ahsahta Press at Boise State University.
Cover and book design by Janet Holmes.
Third printing by Bookmobile in Minneapolis, Minnesota.

AHSAHTA PRESS
2006

Janet Holmes, director
Christopher James Klingbeil
Erik Leavitt
Janna Vega
Allison von Maur
Abigail L. Wolford